TO KEEP
THE BLOOD
FROM DROWNING

poems by

Doug Flaherty

SECOND COMING PRESS

Some of the poems in this book first appeared in: *North American Review, Little Magazine, Foxfire, Big Yellow Bust, Apple, Café Solo, Quartet, Cloven Hoof, Hierophant, Abraxas #5, Puerto del Sol, Folio, Poetry Northwest, Road Apple Review, Greenfield Review,* and *Wind.*

"Raspberries" first appeared in *The Nation.*

"Lake Flies" appeared in *Heartland II,* edited by Lucien Stryk, Northen Illinois University Press, 1975.

"The Forest" appeared on a postcard published by the Bellevue Press, New York.

Cover photograph by Julie Scheinman.

This book was made possible by a grant from the National Endowment for the Arts, Washington, D.C.

SECOND COMING PRESS
P.O. Box 31249
San Francisco, CA 94131

For Tom McKeown

1. BACK TRAILING

RESURRECTION SONG

The belly of corn crib
gives itself to starlings
Feel the almost touch

of hands salute the bees
while a meteor plummets
into a waiting well

Dew blooms to fire
and roots turn to glass
When spring sighs

in the rafters
a golden eel
fills your skull

And night comes again
to bless the light

RAINBOW

While out for pheasant
I turn for home in rain
and catch the sun through water
shooting a rainbow
over the greenhouse
graveyard of red carnations

later at night walking
dreaming of a fist full
of feathers in a girl's hair
I wish I could find
where the rainbow touched down

Or even point to its shadow

WINTER CATCH

A fox paw gnawed clean
to gain the body's freedom
I follow the freshest path
strung-out like clots surfacing
from the stomach of a giant
Pointed in all directions
I am a compass   crazed
by the magnetic field of blood

His innards hollowed by hope
like logs he flees through
The earth a cold moon's reflection
dotting a frozen desert of soul
The Word forbidden the unclean
The paw a relic in a clear jar
nearly prayed to at night

I await the claws to scratch
in distress on the glass
like a head holding a final plea
as it rolls from the blade
needing human hands
pressing to comfort flesh

Tell-tale spoors
like the pox break over
the skin of those who search
secrets in the melting snow

WHILE BUILDING A DOGHOUSE FOR PIPPA, I THINK OF AN OLD MAN SPEAR-FISHING ON LAKE WINNEBAGO

All day he huddles
within his body
within earth within lake
frozen death-blue off-shore
We will never return we think
The prancing blonde paws of dog
tell us we are built by four
north south east west
tell us what the table
tells us and chair tells us
one two three four
Prance says the dance of flesh
The cold line freezes intestines
stringing us back to the cave
Prance to all compass points she says
The old man cuts the line
With a spear he cautions sturgeon
Swigging brandy pulling a long face
he waits to shaft his reflection
Seventy pounds of looming cold
a second across his round mirror
Hammer and nail and t-square
Prance-a-prance and spear down
The tail of lost vision sleeks
its phantom breath across our lives
We were spawned in these waters
breath-washed upon this shore
Prance-a-prance and all fall down
Words are blood-barbed spears
treking us to the stars

RASPBERRIES

The fathers told us
how sparrows
ate a fill of berries
beat wings   dropped
seeds across river
and years of growing
parted by waters
grew into flaming briar

If we believe
what the fathers say
about seeds cleansed
in dark stomachs
and if we start out
heading due north
knifing our bodies
against the current
we will fill a bucket
by last light of today

if we believe
in the guts of words
roots contained in seed
then we will know
that the sparrow
is a bullet
in the heart
of the living dead

BACK TRAILING

for my father

I once carved this tree
It takes me back
thirty years beyond what
it was I started
he told the boy

I know this birch
where I carved initials
the man said again
back trailed a way
set off round the sprawl
of elms and rangy maples

We serve by going back
he said the first time
and turned his wish bone
legs like a divining rod
back to that same birch

I swear to the mad gods
this is the spot I marked
Red-faced out of breath
he sliced with pen knife
the white milky flesh

Letters in reverse clung
and would not run away
He rolled the message
told the boy to follow
back trailing out
of deep woods toward home

BEFORE BIRTH

after Enrique Molina

My mother's heart
thunder in the dark regions
a drum above my skull
in the membranes of soil

I touched only
a deep country of sponges
I was the magic the idol
I lived in an egg of flames

Outside everything was the enemy
the fingernails the voices
the light the forgetfulness
of sprouting seed

I grew luminous eyes of moss
I was a seed full of stars
who kissed you in the womb
slept in a land of red feathers

I was your flesh and your exile

RETURN HOME

I trade kisses shaded by secrets,
and walk with parents through
acres of geraniums and hollyhocks.
We joked about overturned victory gardens
and bombs that escaped our sector.

They once hoed potatoes there
shaded beneath a high stone wall
as I lifted my arms in consecreation.
The sun wove light years of webs
through my fingers and stuck.

How to tell them, how to break
through a half-century of innocence
to bend down a head and whisper:
Loved ones, the world beyond the door
you never heard, or saw, or spoke of.

In this other world a man faces
his summer girl. She clutches a dress
he never touches, pleads to like a child.
Nights, he steals into his stable,
solicits the cold, wet kiss of his pony.

FISH FRY

Beneath the hook-laced mouth
the gray dapple eye tilted.
The world closed as if
all secrets had been answered.

Fish bit when the barometer's high,
when the moon is full.
Is the ritual theirs or ours?
We cast and wait.

They come by weather,
whim, or need. Fish fry.
Chiggers in the grass
burrow in flesh where we scratch.

We eat, and our eaten. Cannibals.
Eat and be sated. But the stare.
We tease loose the hook;
the eye surrenders its light.

The fins stop fanning
like dead butterflies.
The cleft gray eye is buried along
with fins, bones, entrails.

Campfire glows a lake of eyes
asking why bones take on flesh
to be tempted,
set upon, to die.

ARRANGEMENTS

In the year of dog
the sea tumbles fire
rooted deeper than stone
Each village door is an eye

and marriage is arranged
between sun and flower
While trees pray
at the feet of water

candles on the hilltop
the whale on his pillow
informs the landscape
all there is of whiteness

The mole deep beneath skin
touched by the moon's warmth
Through the halo of light
the smudge of ambergris

ANIMALS, BIRDS, and BUGS

1

Raccoons sent up
claws like bent tongs
to clang on garbage cans

Creatures with masks
ancient translators of
the evil beneath our scalp

of our tossed out mail
the secrets of underwear
the intestines of chickens

Behind masks they hide
knowledge we dare not speak
We pare down our nails

to forget what he uncovers

2

The blackbird glides
howls down
the sleet tracks

He drops seed
cleansed
by the threshing wind

*He knows
the preciousness
of mice and weeds*

For hours he drifts
drops seed which blaze
into fruit for my stomach

I squat to leave seed for blackbird

3

Body thin as straw
The larva burrows
eating wood

leaving a sawdust trail
Wanders for years toward
the heart of oak

If only I could
learn to hollow outward
hollow a home

knowing in the guts
how to accomodate
the creature I will be

years beyond my gnawing

4

The jumping bean
taps
at my heart

If he only knew
he worked his way to death
he would be still

But his tapping becomes
the thunder of night
By morning the silence

tears my body open

THE AIR TONIGHT IS THE SMELL

of olive oil and ginger
The girls ready their skin
for the dance in the square

and even the purple neon
pulses in its strange blood
The dark temples of hay loft

flowers on breasts
of young girls who steal
glances at garter snakes

lazed in the deep damp hay
A trail leads nowhere
if anyone forgets to dance

on ground remaining
to be combed and aroused
Before seeds can fall

and open wells conceive
the difference between
water and milk

ON A PASTEL SUMMER DAY

a lady from town
bends to her easel
colors the lawn
the Cape Cod and garage
the zinnias the hollyhocks
But her eyes overlook
the hidden country boy
swaddled in sunlight
the grizzle and tan terrier
nosed in the cool dirt
of laurel and lilac

Her sleight of hand
forgets the monolithic wall
ancient as Indian maize
the wild cherries dipping
with pits and moisture
The woman raises her
yellow chalk hand
oh so ceremoniously

Behind her eyes
a dandelion head
flounced and fragile
as a dry winter snow flake
floats out of her world

2. LANDLADY OF DREAMS

STROKE OF EARTH BLOOD

Carlsbad, N.M. 1973

You say beginnings,
but bring comet tails—
red strokes of earth blood.

Then we enter deep caverns,
wet drop of lime
swells into balls & breasts.

When we ascend into heat
our bodies are beached ships
bloated in afternoon's hot kiss.

Hollow as a flute
we sing into night sleep—
cool whispers thin as wind.

GETTING LOST

For Anick, Valentine's 1975

This is the month of redness
pumping a breast full of blood
You have woven our lives
in a nest hidden in
the farthest tree of forest
It is as St. Robert said
the guide has at heart
our getting lost

The right ones must get saved
We hide and seek the pond
of lost coins and dreams
I want to find that delicate
stillness at the center
The hurricane must supply
the metaphor and quiet space
to ride out all terror

It could have been the womb
but that was ancient history
floating in a raft bobbing
salty seas for months
Our eyes are sheets of glass
both sides touched by
fingerprints of light
hearing all I see into shape

WEDDING SONG FROM THE EAST

We met between words
going backward
into life, into love.

It is not yet my hour.
I am stilled by dictate
of ritual.

I echo my name,
and promises, over and over,
like a wave's rehearsal.

The sea is, for all rhythm,
only water—
no matter how wind,

rocks, sun seduce in its bed.
We drift gently
on saliva of promises.

A hundred feet deep—
buds lay anchor,
take root, and hold.

The tides outrun themselves.
All our lives surviving
behind oceans of mirrors

heaving images,
lugging our future
on their black backs.

LANDLADY OF LOVERS

for Anick

You stare at your hands
at the holes of darkness
through which stars are born

Each pore a room
for a tattered lust-beggar
an asylum for water

You sit by the earth's edge
dripping rivers of water
Deep in your stomach
trout wash the warm fluids

Each lover scrapes
sweat and dirt
from his skin for you
to mold into new tenants

They swim while bobbing
your life in their gills
They will teach you to
carry water from the moon

COUNTRY LOVE

Wicklow, Ireland 1972

The mailbox spilled
years of letters
word hungry to spout
the cadence of love

Dandelions are plucked
by girls who dream flying
in the arms of lovers
never touching night

On the seaweed beach
the moon fell like a brooch
from the throat of sky
All night in a beached tent

a young man wrapped with woman
in tongues of pollen
They fed the fabric of pain
rolled in a rosary of sand

MORNING OF THE WORLD

after Jules Supervielle

A horse twitches
his nostrils
neighs as if flying
Encircled by the unreal
he surrenders to galloping

In the street
the children   the women
like beautiful clouds assembled
to search out their souls

A thousand roosters
lift the countryside
with their song
But the ocean waves
hesitate
between twenty shores

The hour is so dazzled
with men rowing
with fluorescent swimming women
that the stars forget their
reflections
in the speaking water

MISS JULY

Hot sun, dust storm.
Heavy as clouds, the dust.
Suddenly, a full-page nude
floats end-over-end to my feet.
I continue watering the firewheels.

The dust is like smoke.
The girl has seen hard use:
she has come from the arroyo;
her thighs are weltered by earth,
and fine stones, animals perhaps.

She smiles from a face above
large, gourd-like breasts.
Her body, except for the pelvis, is tan.
This has been her summer, moving
from unclad shelter to shelter,
casting one large bright idea.

Now, without domestication,
she comes to a strange man
who has no place for her,
who must water the parched earth.
Keep the sand out of his eyes
the only way he knows how.

WHEN I LOVE YOU IN WOODS

We rub each other fluid
onto sprouting leaf twigs
We steal silently
out of that humid forest bed

to await a clan of leaf people
who will spring from our touch
They would otherwise go naked
without a body-skin of leaves

which they munch to satisfy
the hunger we have borne

STRAWBERRIES

We go to the Cape   at Harwich
Married four years we finally
pick our first meal of sweetness
hidden in the leaf hair of fields
Where you fell over in white jeans
there are red splotches and we laugh

By twilight   burnt by sun   parched
we haul our cargo to the cool kitchen
where my mother hulls and washes
Fingers wave against their bodies
She washes twice again   warns us
that hulled berries tend to bleed

I think about the berries after dark
stumbling about in the pine grove
I stub the intricate shell of a turtle
as she lays eggs   dreams of old tides

MISSOURI WEDDING

All night
the men came
to pin
a forest of greenbacks
on the bride's
gown of seduction

while the groom
lost in a circle
of dancers
awaits the bridal hour

The men touch
all areas
allowable to touch
Concealed
beneath laughter
lies

the dream
for a secret interview
in the lush
foliage of desire

Later
in darkness
the groom sheds
light
enters
her trembling limbs bared

while money
lies crisp but forgotten
on the floor
of her profession

The music quickens
debts unpaid

THE GIRL NOT WITH ME

The mole dreams
the fury of teeth
buzz like saws of wind
Birds like ancient kites
drift asleep off course

Without you five months
I open a door into nothing
It is the same coming back
between a frame of elms
where an old hag weaves walls
and floors of black yarn

Soon the wind forgets to whoop
her crafty children home
On that day the mole will sleep
with the hawk and wonder why
The hag continues spinning
a wall of hands between us

She tends a dozen stray cats
who suck out my breath
I live in twenty black rooms
no soul has ever entered

TO KEEP THE BLOOD
FROM DROWNING

1

Our words hang, rooted
in air, mixing
with small animals.

They come to us
like coffins—
refuge of thought,

gnawing at the door,
caught in the moon's
clicking eye

drinking the night dry.

2

The torment of clock
ticks to a green parrot.
Deer sleep in the grove.

while I hold
an orange to my ear.
The seeds tick

like a lost cloud
Diamonds growing
in the deer's stomachs

shatter with the new tide

3
The world is
out of its element,
no longer the stomach

of your endless trail.
It buoys you before sun,
between air and air

Bones steady water between
your womb, the sea's will.
In spite of hardness, love floats

to keep the blood from drowning.

4.
In this darkness
you are dreaming—
awake or asleep.

You find yourself
crawling on all fours
outside your head,

speaking to the animals,
informing them in turn
you have lost the way:

that waking is dream
or that the animals
are the flesh of desire

There is no darkness like
darkness beneath the black cat
sharpening his claws

on the bones of shadows.

5

These daydreams
(where Raggedy Ann & Andy
caught their childish feet)

are as we ourselves
wild mustangs
munching sweet fern

We will pass this field
again in childhood
to free the improbable ones

The red bees are gathering
sweet death from your lips.
Oh please teach us how.

They suck blood from the sun.

3. MARRIAGE OF WIND AND FEATHERS

TONGUE

Sometime amid dream's waking
ancestors wagging old tongues
split open my stomach
They strung-out my intestines
nailed to a cross-limb
There a fork-tongued snake
rubbed his skin off by the years

They trained my blood to speak
as the tired skin laid bare
quivered like honed metal
On the final circling
I lapped blood against thirst
to translate the garden into bloom

I await the flight of the eagle
the complete man to emerge
from a coat of bear skin
I await the dance of the season
to crush the crystals of death
I seek that land where voices
stir the still waters of caves

APPROACHING THE NATIVITY

for Anick

I hold you all night
under sheets of snow
The cold is a promise
told in icy breath
each night for light years
to keep stars in their place

You freeze your hand
waving greetings so deep
into spring the spiders
will know what to weave
Each snowflake a universe
a picture of your womb

The owl reads your step
holds you in his great eye
You are the blood veins
of all fallen leaves
the gills of fish
breathing frozen words

The doe with hoof in air
cocks her head to hear
strange druid vibrations
coded on your tongue
The mole on your hand
beamed by a cosmic ray

Pockets of snow crouch
They are fluffy hives
full of hungry bees
Their buzz the world's fear
secret dark and deep
That gnawing hum

at the bone marrow
It is the bone
hungry for its own meat
Pack light
The winter will be long

SACRIFICE OF THE STORY BOOKS

There was a time
when the wolf came calling.
Dragonflies broke
from the hearts of hailstones,

and the octopus
rode the plumes of vines.
When time came to pass,
carved by the chip of watches,

men flew above the clouds
in ticking beaked machines
and poked black cavities
in the womb of earth.

In the oven-heat of fields
strawberries froze at the bone.
The old folks prayed aloud.
Cows turned inside out.

Everyone shriveled in flesh
and their bones curved
outside their bodies
in a rainbow toward heaven.

In a cave of words
the final bullet of the world
hangs suspended
by an invisible thread.

LAVA SLEEPS

You pick cranberries
red as the tips of your breasts
Day closes on your hand
while I chase a rabbit
to close the light on flesh

The trees begin to rake
the wounds of leaves
and from your wheelbarrow
you drop berries
to all animals in particular

An empty beehive falls
to shape the sting
your hands have forgotten
Your white dress deserves more
touch than a forest's doormat

I am the beggar of cranberries
I stain you with bright blood
When you smile
lava sleeps
in the mouths of skeletons

TREE KOAN

What is a tree?
Hard flesh with arms and crotches.

Why does a tree have crotches?
To catch the wind's desire.

Is the wind promiscuous?
It loves all trees equally.

Does a tree ever keep the wind?
The tree has learned not to covet.

But doesn't the tree possess ground?
Its feet are rooted in love.

But don't roots run free?
They run to water and embrace.

Then isn't the tree unfaithful to wind?
Secrets are best nurtured in the dark.

But isn't the tree unfaithful?
No tree ever walked away from love?

DEEP ROOTS

1

A cold wind breaks
in the orchestra of winter
while a mouse plucks
the harp strings of a cobweb

2

In step
with winter death
the snowman's ghost
trips over the moon's shadow

3

Icicles are frozen breath
of wildebeests
Children who lick them
turn savage

4

Stars freeze to evergreens
so deep rooted
murmuring
they are earth's veins

BULL FROGS CROAK THE MATINS

to remind the neighbors
of other deaths beside drowning
Crumpled corn stalks test

the manure of the graveyard
townspeople generously supplied
They have a direct telephone

to a country they never found
The bugs arrived first
Children rustle the apple trees

and learn of lizard's welts
rubbing their tender bodies
over bumps of sprouting buds

NIGHT IS AN OLD LADY

unlacing her corset, cropping
darkness from her thighs,
thick with deceit like blinders.
Behind the slaughter house for lambs,
beauty dressed-out in death's clothing.
All the rifles wear silencers
so death cannot be heard.

Suffering stalks
lithely as a greyhound.
The spiders are loose again,
tangle and sting.
Stomachs swell with prey.
Even the owls moan only one syllable—
nature's broken record in a wooden cage.

At daybreak, Night slowly
sucks darkness round her innards.
From out the birth-stench of animal,
a hundred white butterflies
float out the rent eye-sockets
of a gutted spring lamb.

They fan into daydreams— prayer
for mute creations of the womb,
before sky lowers on their thighs
to eat the flesh promise made.
Before fingers of darkness
stir us in a circle of lies.

MARRIAGE OF WIND AND FEATHERS

1

Wind taught the branch
a lesson in motion
The crow settled winter
beneath wings of ice

Stars enter our bodies
smooth as dusk
riding the mare's back

Later in darkness
seeds bless the crow
He not often touches
armor of the turtle

Marriage of wind and feathers
serves the darkness best

2

In a wide circle of grass
a bear clawed bones
sharp as thirst

His sway-arm dug worms
tossed in a moon mouth
Earth joined in the stomach

His moist forehead
sparks behind the eyes
Green becomes red

if looked at long enough
Dust in the throat of hunger
is the taste of blood

3

The sparrow is caught
in the web of thighs

Ice sleeps in its shroud
a winter home of flesh

What we paint here
is food for starvation

This is morning where
no sun dares set foot

Sound becomes prey
We will not walk far

with field mice buried
in their own lime

4

Sun dozes on the sofa
In the hands of silence
the ground whistles

The fluorescent river
rings like a tower bell
not pulled for forty years

The house begins to sway
windows burst into sand
It is then you know

the sound of your footstep
Open the door into yourself

5

The sheep sleep
on altars of goldenrod
Their teeth smile
like worn shoes

Their rich wool
camouflages
a nest of stars
weaving a winter coat

But no guarantee
against loneliness
A homesick ghost
wraps a cord of salt

around the hungry
waist of the moon

6

The water broke
in late afternoon
and shy oars bow
low as a welcome

The red hands
pull back the dark
Recite the family name
dark as a litany

The cord choked
the babe in womb
set him adrift
in a soundless cave

The water murmurs
Death is everybody's darling

7

Back of my head
a mouse climbs a spiderweb
toward a cloud of weeds

Back of my hand
a stream opens warm to release
a trout yanked inside out

Deep mountain light
thirsts after the tongue
Ice crazes the eyes

Suddenly a fox disturbs my supper

8

A holly berry drops
shakes the glazed flakes

Rabbits underground
dream of earthquakes

They strap me to their bones
like a well-worn coat

Deep in the pockets
cold fingers bare words

BLIND SPOT

On any seasonal evening
I lie down on my shadow
and roll closed eyes
gently across my horizon

The black blind spot
shaped like a tunnel
viewed at a mile distance
floats across my sky

The heart talks to itself
as I steady my eyes
and belly-crawl slowly
toward the waiting mouth

The body drags into daylight
trailing its black umbilical
as two fingers bend down
to close the lids on death

THE LAKE FLIES
OF WINNEBAGO

swarm off the cool water
love up against the sun—
side of houses far inland
I think of the abbot Kwaisen
and his monks by free will
burnt alive by mad soldiers

So that even when Yen-t'ou
screamed as the skin bubbled
lungs filled with white
smoke of his own flesh
his scream was heard in
the distant folds of mountain

My mouth clogs with flies
as it opens surprised to tell you
the marauder lake flies have
come to test our will
descend upon us clothed
in spirit wings of old monks

Even later safe indoors
a cup poured for us both
the flowered sheets turned down
they whine and nudge
so deep the window
is dark by noon

THREE-HEADED DOG

All night my life is carried
on the triple tongue of wolf

on the back of the wind
in grains of sand within sand

All night I have hacked
his three yelping heads

to loose from flesh
the language of blood

First head says to read
fate from my intestines

my womb spun from the
path of all fortune

The second head tells me
to smell the trail of woman

and be born each cycle
as father to myself

I have waited for years
like mad monks in caves

without a stock of grain
the chrysalis of prayer

Each new day floats
butterflies without wings

Mother of fishers-of-men
ready the final birth-mark

while the third head mimes songs
which only the wind-eaten sphinx

could decipher from stones
trapped forever like gossip

I dream of hermit days
on the shore of Atlantis

where even fish hooks
are tame as white feathers

All last night hailstones
beat the dark earth clean

like burned-out planets
ovaries of cold birth